A GREAT TIME!

BY MASHA SHURIN

White Stag Press

a division of
Publishers Design Group, Inc.
Roseville, CA

ISBN: 978-0-9792583-2-9

Library of Congress Control Number: 2007926355

Creative director: Robert Brekke

Illustrator: Valentin Ginukov

Book design: Chuck Donald

Translator: Alica Barton

English editor: Brian Morris

Author's cover photo: Inna Shpitalnik

White Stag Press

a division of
PUBLISHERS DESIGN GROUP, INC.
Roseville, California
1.800.587.6666
www.publishersdesign.com

Printed in China

dEDiCATiON

В память моей любимой жены Беатрисы Вайнберг.

Любовь моя, ты лучшею была
Кого я знал в подлунном грешном мире.
Своею смертью душу обожгла.
Я твой портрет храню у нас в квартире.

Как я хочу увидеть тебя снова.
Заглянуть в бездонные глаза.
Сказать "ЛЮБЛЮ"-одно лишь слово.
Слово нежное, как чистая слеза.

In memory of my beloved wife, Beatrisa Vaynberg.

I won't ever give up my first true love.
For me, there is nothing in tomorrow
For you passed away and left great sorrow.
And now I feel myself a lonely dove.

I begged from life a most precious price
To be with you through another while
To feel your lips and see your smile
And slowly deeply draw in your eyes.

You used to tell me, "I love you."
And we still belong to each other.
For we were created for each other.
I believe you need me still, as I need you.

Dedication written by Mikhail Vaynberg, a contributor to this book and close friend of the author

CONTENTS

СОЛНЫШКО

Солнышко - солнышко, где твои глазки?
Ты бы читало волшебные сказки ...
Солнышко - солнышко, где твои ножки?
Ты бы бежало к друзьям по дорожке ...
Солнышко - солнышко где твои ручки?
Ты бы раздвинуло хмурые тучки ...
Солнышко, знаешь, тебе повезло!
Не каждый умеет дарить всем тепло!

SUN

Oh sun. What a shame!
That you do not have eyes,
To see the clouds, the oceans,
and the skies.

Oh sun. What a shame!
That you do not have feet,
To carry you to stars
that you might like to meet.

Oh sun. What a shame!
That you do not have hands,
To build children's castles
or play music with the bands.

But, sun, you are blessed,
and here is why:
You are the most beautiful
thing in the sky!

And not only that,
you love to share, o sun!
You share all your golden rays
with everyone!

But here is the most
incredible part:
You have a large
and generous heart!

It beats and it pulses,
it shines from above,
And fills all the sky
with your light and love.

Your warmth and your kindness,
your radiant grace,
Each day shine down
on every face!

БУКАШКА-ЗАМАРАШКА

Под листиком берёзы
          Сидит роняет слёзы
Пёстрая букашка
          По кличке - Замарашка.
Ей дали эту кличку
          За глупую привычку:
Швырять всё там и сям,
          Не мыться по утрам ...
Ах, лучше бы букашка
          Звалась бы - Обаяшка!

YUCKY THE BUG

A bug sat beneath a shady leaf.
She cried and cried with no relief.
Feeling so lonely and unlucky,
For she was the bug they called "Yucky."

She tried and tried but could never guess,
Why the word *yucky* described her best.
Tho' she picked her nose and made a
          mess
By getting mud all over her dress.

She might have been nicknamed some-
          thing sweet,
If only she learned to wash her feet.
Of course, the reason the nickname stuck,
Was because of bad habits, not bad luck!

ГОРОШКИ

В саду на дорожке
лежали горошки,
Но их потихоньку
склевал воробей.
Ах, если б горошки
имели бы ножки!
Они б по дорожке
умчались скорей.

PEAS

In a garden by the bay,
Pods of green peas aimlessly lay.
Until one warm and sunny day,
In flew a big, hungry blue jay.

The jay pecked the peas while they
had not one word to say.
No fins to swim into the bay,
No legs on which to run away.

They had no choice but to stay,
And be a blue jay's lunch that day.

Про Котика Тимошу

На дворе дождливая осенняя погода ...
А котику Тимоше исполнилось два года.
Несмотря на дождик, две подружки-мышки
Принесли Тимоше новенькие книжки.

Кролик-попрыгунчик, серенький дружок,
Подарил Тимоше вкусный пирожок.
А щенок Лукаша, тоже друг Тимошин,
Вспомнил о погоде и принёс калоши.

Раз в году бывает праздник - День рождения,
Гости и Тимоша - в отличном настроеньи!
На дворе дождливая осенняя погода ...
Котику Тимоше исполнилось два года.

TIMMY THE CAT

It was a wet and windy day in the Fall,
That Timmy the Cat called the best day
    of all!
It was his birthday, a great holiday,
That brought all his friends over to play.

They brought him presents wrapped
    with bows,
To show they loved him more than he
    knows.
The mice gave him cheese and a good
    book to read,

The puppy brought boots and a coat he'd
    need,
And his rabbit friend who liked to bake,
Gave him a special birthday carrot cake!

After Timmy blew out the candles and
    made a wish,
They played with yarn and ate tuna fish.
And though outside the weather was gray,
Timmy and his friends had a wonderful day!

ХОРОШЕЕ НАСТРОЕНИЕ

Архитектор-паучок
        сплетает паутину.
Профессор музыки Сверчок -
        играет сонатину.
Шмель мохнатый,
        скрипке в такт,
        крылышками машет.
Майский жук - большой чудак-
        польку рядом
                пляшет.

A GREAT TIME

One afternoon in early June,
On a warm and sunny day,
The insects threw a party,
Inviting everyone to play.

To start, the cricket fiddled
A melody about the moon.
Then the fuzzy bumblebee
Began to sing along, in tune.

Meanwhile the ladybug swayed,
Her mind so full of romance.
And the beetle joined in,
Doing some sort of polka dance.

They sang, danced, and played,
Yes, each and every one.
The bugs had never guessed,
A party could be such fun!

16

ПРО СЛОНЁНКА, КОТОРЫЙ ХВОСТ ПОТЕРЯЛ

По джунглям скучный брёл
слонёнок.
Он и плакал и вздыхал ...
Хоть и слон, но всё ж – ребёнок.

Хвостик где-то потерял!
Встретит мама у порога
И начнёт его корить.
Папа только скажет строго:
"Без хвоста нельзя ходить!"
Недалёк заката сполох.
Вдруг в кустах раздался шорох.
Серый выскочил мышонок.
Испугался слон-ребёнок ...
"Ты чего, дружище, скучный?
Ты от мамы не отстал?"
И "безхвостик" злополучный
Всё мышонку рассказал.

NO-TAIL, THE ELEPHANT

Walking through the jungle wild,
A baby elephant, a mere child
Let out a loud teary wail:
"Help me, please! I've lost my tail!"

He knew what his mom would say,
"No dessert for you today!
For how could you fail
To notice you misplaced your tail!"

His father, too, would frown and scold,
And then the elephant boy would be told,
"My boy, check the forest trail
before your name becomes 'No-Tail'."

While the sun was bright in the sky,
No-Tail heard a noise nearby.
A rustling came from a tiny house,
Out of which popped a little mouse.

The mouse said: "I see your eyes,
And from inside I heard your cries
As I listened to you wander about,
I wondered if I could help you out.
Tell me, what is bothering you?
Maybe there's something I can do.
I may not be big, I may not be wise,
But I am helpful, despite my size!
I'll be a friend to you right now,
And try my best to help somehow!"

Continued on next page…

So, No-Tail told the mouse all about
His tail and how he came to be with-
    out.
"That's not a problem," the mouse
    replied,
"My tail is long, and for you, just right.
So don't be sad." With a big smile he
    said,
"In place of your lost tail take mine,
    instead!"

The elephant child was so surprised,
Though he saw it with his own eyes!
"I just don't understand, you see,
Why you would do this, all for me?"

It might sound a bit absurd,
But I did it for a special word:
It's *Friendship*," the mouse said.
"I found a friend and I am so glad!"

This little word brings joy,
To every animal, girl, and boy.
It gives a hand to hold, a life to share,
A hug from friends to show they care.

Now you know and don't forget,
He gave his tail with no regret.
Elephant replied, "for all you do,
I'll be your best friend forever, too."

Тут мышонок рассмеялся-
"Успокойся, не грусти!
Коль без хвостика осталась,
Мой возьми, вот, и носи ..."
Слово "дружба" есть на свете,
Слово очень не простое.
Знать его должны все дети,
Слово нужное такое.
В нём и радость и веселье.
В нём и счастье и покой ...
Не должно быть тут сомнений -
Будем мы дружить с тобой!
Солнца луч закатный тонок ...
Распевают в унисон
Добрый маленький мышонок
И большой весёлый слон.

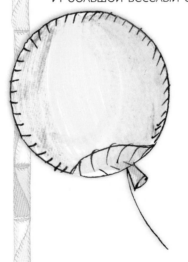

БАРМАЛЕЙ

Далеко в своей избушке
Мастерит сидит игрушки
Очень добрый Бармалей
Только нет вокруг друзей.

Потому, что злые духи
Распустили всюду слухи,
Будто страшный Бармалей
Ест всех маленьких детей.

Только всё это-не так!
Бармалей-чудной добряк!
Любит он цветы и травку,
И лягушку, и ... пиявку.

Очень хочет съесть конфету,
Но в лесу конфеты нету.
Жить он должен не болея.
Жалко-жалко Бармалея.

И один в глуши своей
Очень добрый Бармалей
Мастерит сидит игрушки:
Куклы, санки и вертушки
Всё для маленьких детей.

THE BOOGIE MAN

Day and night in his secret house,
He works as quiet as a mouse,
The kind and loving Boogie Man,
Making toys as quick as he can.

Despite his good work, he has no friends,
Because his reputation tends
To make the Boogie Man into a beast
Who eats children as a nightly feast.

What's the truth?

The Boogie Man loves all things sweet,
Like cookies, ice cream, and trick-or-treats.
He loves a sky lit up with stars,
Kittens, flowers, and shiny cars,
Bright colored laces on his shoes,
Fresh cut grass and barbeques,
Watching waves splash on the sand
And catching raindrops with his hands.

The thought that makes his warm heart
    race,
Is when he thinks of the smiling face
Of a happy girl or a happy boy,
For whom he made his many toys.

Tho' the children believe he's scary,
Green and mean and tall and hairy,
A thing the children would never touch,
The Boogie Man loves them very much.

УЛИТОЧКА

В доме улитки нету дверей.
В нём-никогда не бывает гостей.
Букашки к улитке никак не зайдут,
Не сядут к столу и чайку не попьют.
Гостей своих видит улитка во сне-
Ведь домик свой носит она на спине.

THE SNAIL'S HOUSE

The snail's house has no doors
So her friends can't come in.
All day long she dreams and thinks,
Of how to visit them.

She can't invite the other bugs
To tea or for a snack,
Because her little doorless house,
She carries on her back!

KANGAROO

In down under Australia
The best mailman is found,
Delivering the mail
To kids in every town.

He hops many a mile
Bearing letters to read,
Always with a smile
Bringing packages they need.
Like candy from India
Where elephants roam,
And shirts from Africa
Where lions call home.

For kids in every town,
You now know to be true,
The best mailman found
Is, of course, the kangaroo.

КЕНГУРУ

В загадочной Австралии
Есть чудный почтальон!
И даже из Италии
Доставит письма он.
А может и посылочку
Детишкам принесёт,

Привет от Санта-Клауса
Под самый Новый Год ...
Доставит всё как следует
И к самому двору.
Вы догадались, дети,
Что это ... КЕНГУРУ.

ЛЯГУШОНОК-БОЦМАН

Крошечный кораблик
        по волнам плывёт,
Лягушонок-боцман
        песенку поёт.
О родном болоте
        с зелёною травой.
Он терерь на флоте,
        он теперь - герой!

THE SAILOR FROG

A little boat is riding free
On the wild and stormy sea.
The captain is a sailor frog

Who guides the boat through storm and
    fog.

The swamps are where he used to roam,
But now he calls the sea his home.
And sails bravely on the big blue sea,
Singing songs of victory!

Грустные Обезянки

Обезянки-манки сидели на полянке.
Сидели и грустили, друг другу говорили.
Мы азбуки не знаем, не пишем, не читаем.
Не можем мы считать. Как нам не горевать?
Мы песенку о дружбе не можем даже спеть.
Ну как нам обезянок таких не пожалеть?

MONKEYS

Monkeys, monkeys in the trees
Asking "Who will help us, please.
The alphabet, we want to learn,
To read and write is our concern."

We can't compose a letter,
Even when we work together.
We can't even sing a song,
On how monkeys get along!
If only we could count to three;
We would live so happily!

Yes, it's really very sad,
That these monkeys cannot add.
Will you help them? Please, please,
    please,
To read and write and count to three.

RUSSIAN POETRY & STORIES FOR CHILDREN

Masha Shurin, a native of Belarus, a republic of Russia, has written stories and poems that have been translated into English for children, ages two to ten. Each book reflects the flavor, artistry, and culture of her native Russian homeland. The series includes four books.

A Great Time

Includes eleven poems about bugs, frogs, elephants, the sun, insects, cats, monkeys, and more. All created to help children learn to be respectful, kind, helpful, and generous.

The Lonely Wizard

This is a story of a lonely wizard who brings life to his hand-made toys. The fairy tale focuses on the power of friendship and cooperation as an eagle and a rabbit help the wizard find his stolen toys.

The Composer Donkey

A collection of short stories about animals and a little donkey who decides to take the lead in composing great music. The stories focus on friendship and leadership with strong, character-building messages.

A Princess Shell

A love story between a prince who lives on land and a princess who lives in the sea. This fairy tale convincingly proves that the power of love can conquer in all situations.

Books may be purchased from your favorite bookstore, online at Amazon.com, or through the publisher at:

White Stag Press, a division of Publishers Design Group, Inc.
P. O. Box 37, Roseville, CA 95678, or by calling 1.800.587.6666

www.whitestagpress.com
or; www.publishersdesign.com